THE BASKETBALL PSYCHOLOGY WORKBOOK

"From Average to Primetime"

Attain the Mental Edge

Dedication

This Workbook is specially dedicated to all the young Basketball Stars of the world. With relentless pursuit, undying passion, and laser focus even your wildest dreams can become a reality.

PREFACE

In todays' basketball world there are (overall) 4 types of players. Here's what those are:

1. *Talented Players* who are *Ambitious* to Learn how to Improve
2. *Non-Talented Players* who are *Ambitious* to Learn how to Improve
3. *Talented Players* who have *No Ambition* to Learn how to Improve
4. *Non-Talented Players* who have *No Ambition* to Learn how to Improve

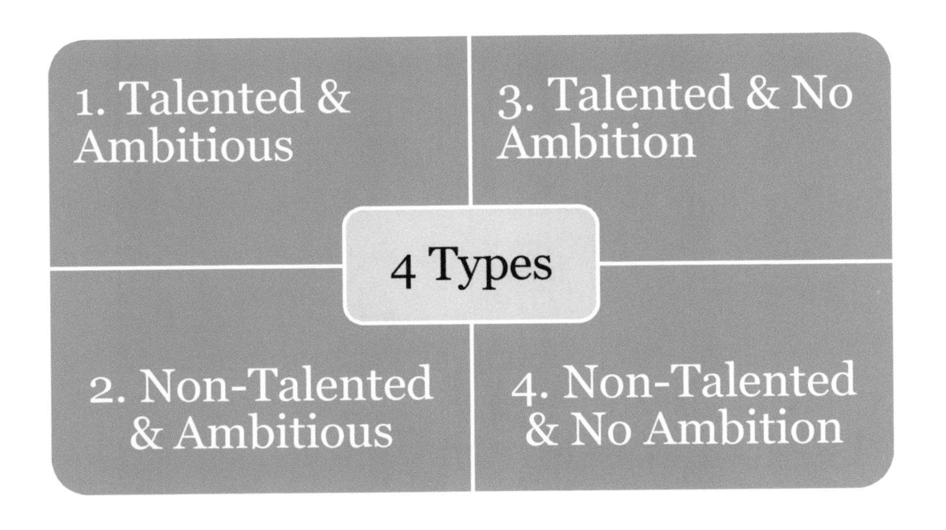

Being born with Talent or Not is something that is really out of the Athlete's control... but having the Ambition to Learn and Improve is completely something that we have the power to influence. Why do I make this a point? Because many of the basketball athletes I speak to on a daily basis get caught up in the idea that Talent automatically equals success on the court. That Talent is the answer to all problems. That Talent makes it "Easy." That Talent nearly guarantees the college scholarship everyone is after...And this couldn't be further from the truth. Although Talent does predispose some athletes to be more skilled and enables them to learn a lot faster than others....the truth is that the real reason athletes become successful is because they possess the ambition to learn and improve and actually go out and put in the work! It is 1000% possible for an athlete to have zero basketball talent but work their tail off to achieve massive success.

However, with that being said let's get something straight right off the bat. If you're picking up this workbook with the expectation of finding some sort of short-cut...some sort of secret formula...some sort of magic potion you can use that will allow you to bypass all the hard work and effort that's required to become successful on the basketball court, you're simply Wasting Your Time! You won't find it here and you won't find it anywhere else, because it just doesn't exist.

The fact is that without the Ambition to Learn and Improve and the Desire to put in the work your results will continue to be mediocre. And our aim isn't for you to be a mediocre player. In fact, this Workbook is geared specifically to those of you in the 1st and 2nd quadrants only, meaning whether you are naturally talented or not you're without question eager to work hard and eager to learn how you can get better in any way, shape, or form.

Now, for purposes of clarity this workbook has one goal, and only one goal in mind: TO IMPROVE YOUR BASKETBALL PERFORMANCE. How will we accomplish this? Well, we will do this by showing you how your thoughts and mindset have a direct impact on how well you perform on the basketball court. We will give you deep insight as to how your inner emotions and thoughts can leave you vulnerable to consistently under-performing which in turn can lead to anger, frustration, and disappointment. Along the way, you will learn the mental skills that many of today's great athletes use to propel themselves ahead of their competition. You will learn what it takes to perform your best under intense pressure, you will learn how to overcome crippling adversity, you will learn how to cope with pre-game nerves and anxiety, you will build mental toughness, and you will learn to develop supreme confidence in your abilities. As the rest of the world is just now realizing "Physical Skills are important, but Mental Skills are what separates Champions from the Rest of the Pack."

TABLE OF CONTENTS

- How will Mental Imagery Influence my Athletic Performance?

4. **Thought Suppression**: "The Truth of the Matter is that Thought Suppression is a Lot Like Not Studying Before a Big Test, You're Simply Setting Yourself Up for Failure"

- What is Thought Suppression?
- How does Thought Suppression impact my basketball performances?
- What are some strategies to avoid Suppressing my Thoughts?

5. **Competitive Anxiety**: "You Never Reach your Full Potential because you Let Fear Control your Thoughts, and those Fearful Thoughts Create Fearful Emotions, and those Fearful Emotions Lead to Fearful Actions"

- What is Competitive Anxiety?
- How does Competitive Anxiety affect players differently?
- How can I learn to control my Anxiety to play better?

6. **Self-Talk**: "Self-Talk has been Shown to be an Incredibly Powerful Psychological Skill that is Used by Some of the Most Successful Athletes on the Basketball Court"

- What is Self-Talk?
- How can Self-Talk help me perform better on the basketball court?

- What are the different types of Self-Talk?

7. **Zones of Optimal Performance**: "Reaching a Mental Zone is Difficult, but When Accomplished Many Ballers Describe the Ease of the Game, Shooting the Ball Feels Like Throwing a Rock into the Ocean, and Every Move Becomes Buttery Smooth"

   - What is a Zone of Optimal Performance?
   - Where is my level of Optimal Performance?
   - What skills can I utilize to reach my Zone of Optimal Performance?

8. **Attention**: "With so Many Factors Fighting for Your Attention You Become Like a Sniper in the Middle of a Warzone, You Need to be Able to Focus All of Your Attentive Energy on the Things that Matter Most at that Very Moment"

   - What are the different forms of Attention?
   - Why do I have Mental lapses and Attentive break downs?
   - What can I do to have laser like focus?

9. **Self-Confidence**: "You are the Architect, you can Build Yourself Up High Like a SkyScraper or you can set a Flimsy Foundation that can Collapse at any Moment."

   - How can I Build up my Self-Confidence?
   - What are the different factors that can influence my Self-Confidence?

- How can I sustain high levels of Confidence throughout the course of my basketball career?

10. **Coming Back From Injury**: "What Most Athletes Fail to Realize is that the Physical Pain is Intense, but Tolerable, it's the Psychological Pain that Becomes Almost Unbearable to Deal With"

    - What are the Psychological factors involved in Injury Recovery?
    - How can I return from an Injury faster and stronger than before?
    - What are the Physical and Psychological connections when an Injury occurs?

Motivation

"A BASKETBALL PLAYER WITHOUT MOTIVATION IS LIKE A CAR WITHOUT GAS, NEITHER WILL GET VERY FAR."

Mental Meltdown

You're waking up out of bed, 7:00am sharp on a cold December morning. The entire week you've been motivated about becoming a better basketball player and leading up to today you've made the conscious decision to wake up early, put your gym shoes on, grab your bag, and head straight down to the basketball gym to work on your jump shot mechanics. But now that the day has finally arrived... you realize that it's Saturday, it's cold, your body is sore from yesterday's practice, and you're just way too warm and comfortable in your bed at the moment to get up and start your workouts. You hit snooze on the alarm and go back to sleep.

What happen to the overflowing amounts of Motivation you had?

Now let's not get carried away, athletes go through these situations all the time and under certain circumstances it's perfectly okay to get some extra rest. After all the grind of a competitive season brings along a lot of stress on the body that requires some recovery and recuperation time. It only becomes a problem when skipping workouts and not following through with your commitments becomes a habit. And unfortunately this is very, and I mean very, common. Just take a listen to some of the promises your friends and peers make when summer time comes around... "I'm going to lose 20 pounds and get my body summer ready... I'm going to diet and eat nothing but fruits and vegetables for the next two weeks... I'm going to wake up early every day and go to the gym."

Fast forward to a few months later and guess what? Absolutely nothing has changed! No diet, no weight loss, and of course no early morning gym sessions. To get to the point, without a true sense of motivation it becomes extremely difficult to get things done. And when you're an aspiring athlete this makes all the difference. To become successful on the court it's crucial that you identify what your underlying motivation is so that you can feed off of it and use it to fuel your efforts.

Definition & Examples

Motivation: your "reason", your "why" of what you practice for and what you work hard for.

Example

1. "I'm staying late after practice today to work on my jump shot." Why am I staying late? Because I want to be a better shooter than my older brother. So my motivation is beating and performing better than my older brother.

   Little Known Fact: Motivation as a whole goes a whole lot deeper, and here's a quick breakdown. There are actually two different types of motivation... Intrinsic Motivation and Extrinsic Motivation.

Intrinsic Motivation: motivation that comes from within you or from inside of you.

Example

1. "I have a passion and a love for basketball. I don't need any extra attention from people or any special prizes to keep playing, I simply enjoy playing the game."

Extrinsic Motivation: motivation that comes from something outside of you.

1. "I like to play basketball because it makes my dad really happy. Also, for every game that our team wins I get a crisp $20 bill, this keeps me driven to play my best.

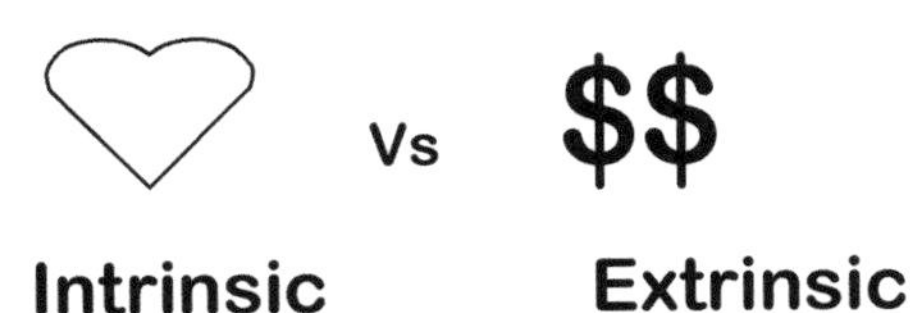

The Game Plan

Simple distinction right? If you didn't understand the difference between the two types please take a moment and re-read both definitions and examples again. Now, you might be wondering which type of motivation is best for maximizing your talents and efforts? And if you guessed Intrinsic Motivation, you are Correct. Here's why.

When your motivation comes from within you, you don't need some external reward or some type of trophy to work hard and give it your all. It's just something that comes natural to you, and you feel a burning desire inside of you to continue to push yourself. You have a passion and a love for basketball, and if you receive anything along the way it's nice to get the recognition but it's not necessary for you to continue to be driven. And the truth is that this is the way most really successful basketball players maintain high levels of performance. When you're watching your favorite players on TV this is difficult to notice because of course they are under the spot light and have all the attention from fans, but what you don't see is the thousands and thousands of hours of practice that go on behind the scenes. And it's no surprise that the best players are the same ones who are the last ones to leave the gym, despite them already knowing they are better than everyone else.

Now on the other hand, when an athlete is Extrinsically Motivated, they may find success in the beginning... but what eventually ends up happening is their motivation starts to slowly fade away which only leads to the athlete "burning out." If you're not familiar with the term Burn Out, it's simply a term used to describe the physical and mental exhaustion of an athlete. Why does this happen? Well, this type of athlete works hard also, but only works hard for the reward, works hard for the trophy, works hard for the scholarship, works hard for the money. Once the athlete acquires these external objects that he/she is motivated in attaining, what's next? What comes after that? What becomes their reason for continued hard work and effort? NOTHING! There aren't any other reasons or desires to want to continue to improve and get better. Since this athlete's sole motivation was to possess that external reward, once it's in their hands they become complacent, comfortable, and un-driven. With that being said, there's no problem with getting recognition for athletic achievement…it's actually something to be extremely proud of and something that should be celebrated. The issue only becomes apparent if you're true underlying goal is to become the BEST.

If I don't win the MVP trophy this season I won't play

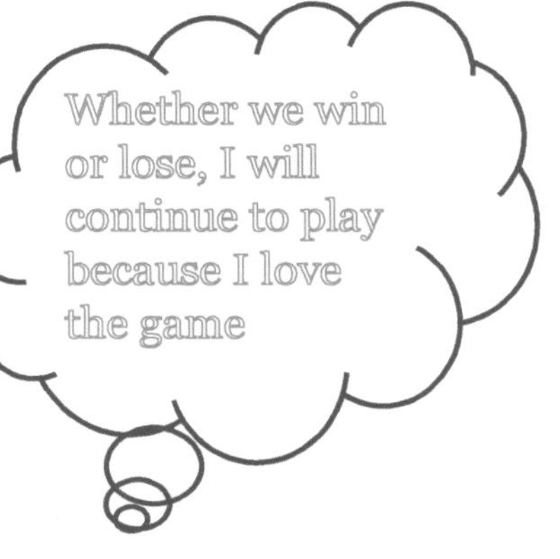

So what's the take away? In order to be successful on the basketball court you need to find your true Intrinsic Motivation. Find your Why. Find your reason. And make sure it's something that makes YOU happy, NOT someone else. Keep that fire inside of you burning for as long as possible, because once it's gone it's very hard to get it lit again.

Mental Workout

1. Write down all the reasons why you play basketball. What's your motivation for playing? Is it Intrinsic or Extrinsic?

____

____

____

____

2. Write down all the reasons why you think you feel motivated one day, and unmotivated the next day. What types of distractions do you have around you? How can you avoid these distractions from getting in the way of your success?

3. Talk to your friends and teammates and see if you can find what drives their motivation. Can you tell who is Extrinsically Motivated and who is Intrinsically Motivated?

Goal-Setting

> *"NOT SETTING GOALS IS LIKE PLAYING A GAME WITHOUT KEEPING SCORE, YOU CAN'T REALLY TELL WHETHER YOU'RE WINNING OR LOSING."*

Mental Meltdown

Imagine this... You wake up from a long nap and find yourself alone in a car with no phone or any type of technology in sight. You're headed on a long road trip to a small town that you know is somewhere to the North of you but you have no directions as to how to get there. You really have no idea how far this place is or how long it should take you to get there.

What are you to do?

This example is a little far-fetched (as you will probably never be put in this position), but it makes the perfect point: YOU CAN'T REALLY KNOW WHERE YOU'RE GOING WITHOUT A CLEAR ROADMAP! And a goal is exactly that, a roadmap to reach your desired level of success. For some odd reason however, many of today's youth athletes really have no desire to create clear and concise goals. Which leads to the questions... Where are you going? How will you get there? When will you get there? What do you need in order to arrive on time?

The Best Athletes know what they want, they understand exactly what it will take to get there, and they know how long it will take them to get there. It's not a very complicated process to understand, but there are some Key factors you need to be aware of in terms of learning proper goal setting techniques. Once you get these strategies down, you'll be light years ahead of your peers and will drastically improve your chances of success!

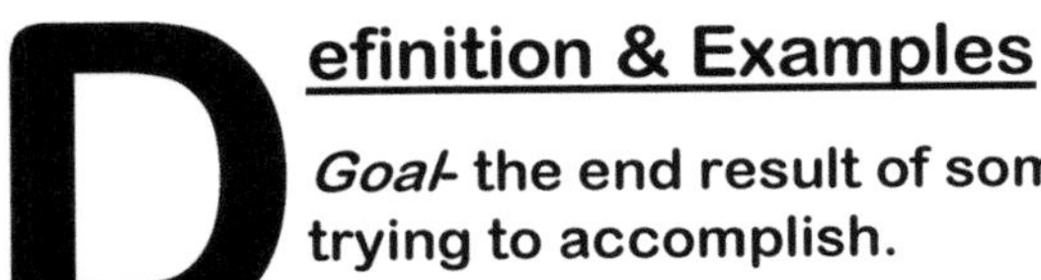

Definition & Examples

Goal- the end result of something you are targeting or trying to accomplish.

Example

1. "My goal is to be the best basketball player I can be."

Most of the goals you set for yourself are very likely similar to the example given above. Really simple, really generic, and straight to the point. But there's a huge problem with setting goals this way. What's the problem? These types of goals never get accomplished! They never get accomplished because there's no way of measuring any type of progress. Setting a very vague goal doesn't give you the ability to track whether or not you're taking steps forward, taking steps backwards, or staying in the exact same place. The simple solution to this requires the athlete to become more specific, which leads us to our next point...there are two categories when it comes to goal setting: short term goals and long term goals.

Long Term Goal- your main objective/target. (big picture)

Short Term Goal- checkpoints that need to be reached in order to accomplish your long term goal. (small scope)

Example

1. "Two months from now I want to be shooting 80% from the free throw line, that's my long term goal. In order to do that I need to increase my shooting percentage by 5% every month, those are my short term goals. In order to increase my shooting percentage by 5% every month I'm going to shoot 100 free throws every day after practice and I'm going to keep track of how many I make and miss (even more precise short term goals)." The more precise you get, the better.

Week 1

Monday	Tuesday	Wednesday	Thursday	Friday
66%	72%	63%	69%	70%

Overall= 68%

Week 2

Monday	Tuesday	Wednesday	Thursday	Friday
69%	71%	68%	76%	68%

Overall= 70.4%

Week 3

Monday	Tuesday	Wednesday	Thursday	Friday
74%	72%	70%	81%	76%

Overall= 74.6%

Week 4

Monday	Tuesday	Wednesday	Thursday	Friday
79%	75%	73%	81%	71%

Overall= 75.8%

The Game Plan

Okay let's quickly recap. You need to set a long term goal (destination) along with short term goals (specific directions) to help you reach your target level of success. Simple. now let's take it one step further. Whenever you set a long term or short term goal you need to make sure that it's not Too Easy, but not Impossibly Difficult. The level of difficulty that every goal should fall between is right around the moderately difficult category. Take a look at the spectrum that follows.

Goal Setting Level of Difficulties

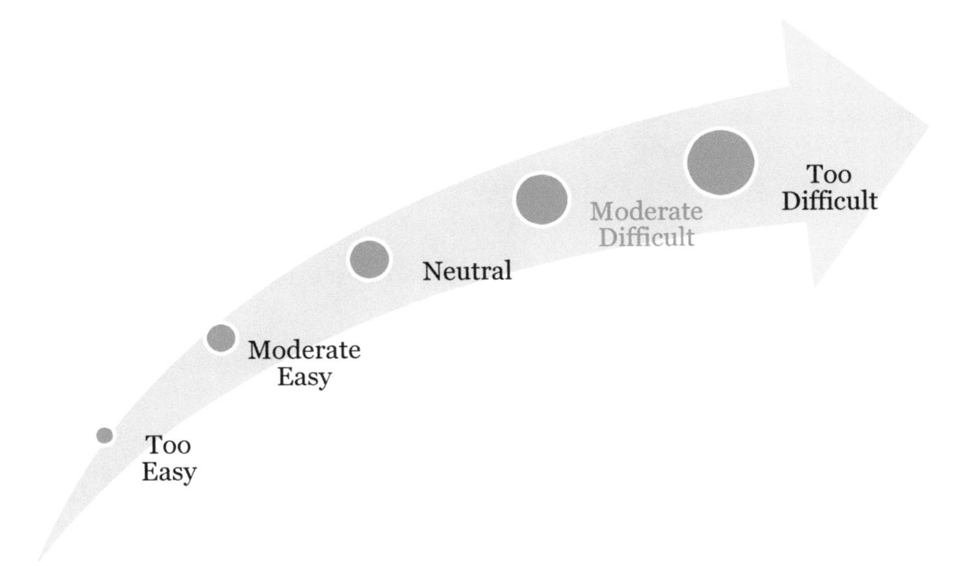

Too Easy- Not at all challenging for you

Moderately Easy- Only a little challenging for you

Neutral- An even balance between easy and challenging for you

Moderately Difficult- Challenging and pushes your Limits

Too Difficult- Overly challenging and difficult to notice any real progress

The magic formula lands in the moderately difficult category for the simple reason that these types of goals challenge you and test your limits but also give you a certain sense of belief that you can accomplish what you've set out to accomplish. Let's consider the other side of the coin. When a goal is too easy it doesn't challenge or motivate you which leads to boredom, and when a goal is extremely difficult it's really hard for you to see any results or progress. Without seeing any results or progress your confidence is shot down to the ground, and will eventually lead to you quitting or giving up. That's the last thing we want.

Finally, something that you absolutely must remember from now on every time you set a goal should incorporate the following characteristics. The acronym is SMART. Here's what it stands for:

Specific: every goal you set must be very specific, clear, and concise.

Measurable: every goal you set must have some measurable aspect to it. If you're looking to become faster you can time yourself, if you want to get stronger you can keep track of how much weight you're lifting.

Action-oriented: every goal should require you to take action whether physically or mentally.

Realistic- as we mentioned before your goals need to be realistic (in the moderately difficult category, not impossibly difficult or incredibly easy).

Timely- all goals need to have a deadline, some sort of time frame to ensure you're doing everything you can to reach your target.

And there you have it, the Proper Goal Setting Techniques. By incorporating all facets: Long Term Goals, Short Term Goals, The Goal Setting Difficulty Spectrum, and SMART…you are equipped to improve your performance to a very high level at a very quick pace. And remember, as you begin to accomplish the goals you've set things will become easier and easier for you, allowing you to modify your goals as you go which will only make you that much better as a player.

ental Workouts

1. Begin now, write down 3 long term goals you want to accomplish.

____

____

____

____

2. Develop a plan and a series of short term goals of how you will accomplish those 3 long term goals. Remember to keep track, whether daily, weekly, or monthly.

Mental Imagery

> *"MENTAL IMAGERY IS A LITTLE LIKE HAVING A MOVIE IN YOUR HEAD, AND SIMPLY HITTING PLAY ON YOUR DVD PLAYER WHENEVER YOU'RE READY TO WATCH IT."*

Mental Meltdown

There's nothing like watching one of those classic and exciting basketball movies. From Hoosiers, to He Got Game, to Glory Road, Above the Rim, Coach Carter, and list can go and on... There's just something special about watching a movie about the sport you love that motivates you to get back in the basketball gym and work your tail off! This may be in part due to the fact that so many of us consciously or unconsciously put ourselves in the role of the main characters in the movie. We take a ride on the emotional roll-a-coaster the film is portraying... we feel the pain, we feel the anguish, we feel the frustration, and at the end we feel the triumph and success when the movie characters pull it together and get the Win in the face of Adversity.

And in actuality, this exact process is a lot how Mental Imagery (also known as Visualization) works! Mental Imagery is like having a movie in your head, and simply hitting Play on the DVD player whenever you're ready to watch it.

Unlike the movies however, in real life things don't always end the way you'd want them to end. For example, after playing a bad game or not performing up to your standards you may think back and begin to run all the costly mistakes you made during the course of the game or across the entire season. You visualize yourself missing open jumpers, forgetting plays, getting crossed over, getting dunked, getting frustrated, getting yelled at, being made fun of, and losing your starting position despite all your hard work and effort. And in doing so you get yourself into a huge "funk" which is the exact opposite of what you wanted in the first place! In order to avoid this from happening, it's crucial you realize that the images you play in your head have an enormously powerful impact on your basketball performance. Learning the proper way to utilize Mental Imagery is vital, and it's important you use it as an advantage instead of as a pitfall so your game can reap the positive benefits.

Definition & Example

Mental Imagery (Visualization)- using your thought processes and imagination to create very detailed images and pictures in your mind. These images can be of past experiences or future moments in the way you would like them to play out.

Example

1. I'm in the driveway practicing my jumper. I close my eyes and imagine the shot clock winding down to 4 seconds. I catch the ball, the crowd is roaring, I can feel the pressure, but I'm confident. I take two dribbles to the right, pull up for a three pointer, I see the ball rotating perfectly toward the basket, I hear the buzzer go off and swish, the ball goes in hitting nothing but the bottom of the net. The crowd goes wild, my teammates are jumping up and down with excitement, I can feel the adrenaline running through my veins, we win the game!

LIGHTS....CAMERA.... ACTION!!

The Game Plan

If you're aspiring to be a great basketball player at some point, then you've most definitely closed your eyes and dreamed about experiencing massive success on the court... about making game winning shots... about making incredible defensive plays.... and gaining all the respect from your friends and peers. And it's perfectly normal, all great athletes do it regardless of the sport they play. What's important however is to realize that the way you process these mental images must be done in an effective and efficient manner. Believe it or not, there is a certain science to it. Here is a check list of components you need to use in order to apply Mental Imagery to your basketball career and maximize your potential.

Before working on your jump shot, before lifting weights, before playing a game, anything that requires a specific skill set or process, take ten minutes and just visualize yourself being successful. Visualize yourself correctly executing every move, every movement, and every step. Imagine every shot you take hitting nothing but net, being so fast that no one can drive past you, being so strong that whatever weight you put on the bar seems light. You're just overflowing with confidence and can handle anything that comes your way. Along this process however, it's important that you be very, and I mean very detailed and specific on the pictures you're running through your mind. Like I mentioned earlier, it should be like playing a movie in your head.

You must use all your senses: touch, sight, smell, hear, taste. As you begin to learn how to incorporate all your senses, you will start to notice that you will progressively feel more and more as if you were presently in the moment you are imagining. And this is what we're aiming for. Because you're envisioning vivid and detailed mental pictures your brain begins to release the exact same chemicals and signals throughout your body as if you were actually in that moment. This will allow you to experience the same emotional responses and phenomenon's you would have as if it were happening in real time, thus allowing you to prepare in advance and give you the feeling as if "You've been there before" when that moment finally arrives.

Example:

Let's say that during yesterday's game you shot 4 for 7 from the free throw line. You know you can shoot better, so before today's game you take ten minutes and visualize yourself successfully executing your routine and swishing every free throw.... "I'm at the free throw line, I can feel the cold sweat drenched onto my jersey, I can hear the crowd chanting for a miss, I can smell and almost taste the popcorn coming from the snack bar, but my eyes are locked in on the rim. The referee throws me the ball...and I go through my usual routine...1 dribble, 2 dribbles, 3 dribbles...I bend my knees, get into my shooting form, smoothly rise up into my shot, snap my wrist down and release the ball in a backward spiral towards the rim...the ball slowly falls directly into the basket hitting nothing but net." And repeat this same process again and again free throw after free throw...elevating your confidence each step of the way.

Learning how to become efficient in the use of mental imagery can be very challenging at times because it's not something that will give you immediate results. So it's important to remember that just like every other skill you've ever learned, you only get better with dedicated time and practice. When you were a baby and first started to learn how to walk it didn't just take you 1 day, it took you weeks, even months to learn how to execute every movement correctly. Don't get discouraged or frustrated in your beginning stages of mental imagery practice, even if you feel like it's not working. Keep practicing, keep getting better, and in time your game will in fact positively benefit.

Mental Workout

1. Follow the steps given in the last few paragraphs. Take a skill you want to be better at, and before practicing or even during practice, envision yourself being successful. Picture yourself doing everything right. Remember to be very specific, think about all the steps, all the movements, and everything around you.

____

____

2. Once you start learning how mental imagery can work for you, start developing a routine. Maybe there's a quiet place that you can visit, a song you can play on your ipod, or a certain time of day when visualizing is more effective for you (in the morning when you wake up, or at night before you go to sleep). Repeat that routine as often as possible. Write your routine down.

Thought Suppression

"THE TRUTH OF THE MATTER IS THAT THOUGHT SUPPRESSION IS A LOT LIKE NOT STUDYING BEFORE A BIG TEST, YOU'RE SIMPLY SETTING YOURSELF UP FOR FAILURE."

Mental Meltdown

You're sprinting down court on a fast break all alone with only seconds remaining on the clock. Your teammate passes you the ball and all you have to do is lay the ball in nice and easy into the basket to put your team in a great position to come away with a win and secure a spot in the playoffs. But...as you gather your steps and take flight...you don't get the elevation you usually do which breaks your concentration for a split second. You try and compensate by laying the ball up off the backboard much higher than you usually do and you end up blowing the lay-up...just missing by an inch with the ball rolling off the front of the rim. Your team loses the game and loses its playoff birth. On the bus ride home you can't help but have the same recurring thought run clear across your mind...

"I DON'T WANT TO THINK ABOUT IT ANYMORE!"

It happens to the best of us...all we want to do is bury that unforgiving memory into the deepest and darkest crevice of our mind and lock it away forever and ever...never to be seen again. We want to get as far away as possible from those traumatizing and overwhelming feelings of despair, frustration, and disappointment.

This type of thought process is called Thought Suppression and it's exactly what many athletes engage in after a poor performance. But is Thought Suppression an effective strategy? Is Thought Suppression the best approach to overcoming a bad performance? What is the result of suppressing your thoughts? Well, in reality Thought Suppression is mentally one of the worst things you can possibly do when it comes to trying to elevate your athletic performance. It's really a lot like not studying before a big test, you're simply setting yourself up for failure.

efinition and Examples

Thought Suppression- attempting to stop thinking about a certain idea, or trying to stop certain thoughts from running through your mind.

Example

1. Let's further consider the same example given in the previous section. You've missed a wide open lay-up at the end of a game and are now on a very long bus ride home. You continue to have the same recurring thought "DON'T THINK ABOUT IT!!!"

   The next day comes and you're still trying your best not to think about it. To aid the process, you try something a little different... every time those unwanted thoughts of the missed lay-up resurface into your consciousness, you attempt to replace those thoughts with other memories that are completely unrelated and unattached. You think about the amazing flavors of your favorite food...you think about your exciting upcoming family vacation...and you think about how nicely those new Jordan shoes fit you. (things that usually help you feel better)

   And guess what??? This is where things get a little confusing, because what starts to happen is that now the unpleasant memory of missing a lay-up becomes linked to your pleasant memories of your favorite food, your family vacation, and your new Jordan shoes. Meaning that every time you think about these pleasant memories...your mind reverts back to that missed lay-up!

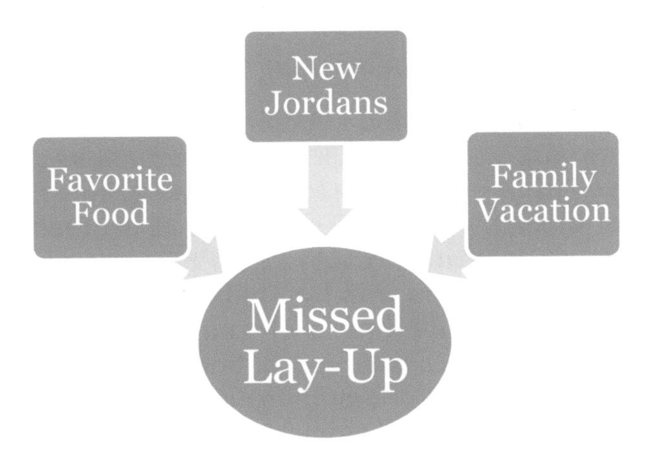

It's difficult to comprehend how this works in the beginning, but it's a very common phenomenon in psychology known as a Rebound Effect.

Thought Suppression Rebound Effect- as you attempt to suppress a thought (not think about it), you actually end up thinking about it even more. Your mind becomes occupied with thinking about the very thought you don't want to think about!

The Game Plan

Since it's a contradicting concept, let's explain in further detail. The way memory works in your mind is by forming links between associated objects or ideas. For example, when someone says the word "dog" what automatically pops into your head? You probably start to think about the words "paws, bark, bite, and fur." The stronger the links are between the associated objects or ideas, the higher likelihood you are to recall those particular memories. And since your mind doesn't distinguish between unwanted memories versus pleasant memories, when it comes to suppressing your thoughts and attempting to replace an unwanted memory with a pleasant memory you're actually associating and forming a bond/link between the two. And this is important to understand as a basketball player or an athlete in general because "DON'T THINK ABOUT IT" often leads to the exact opposite of what your desired goal is...which is to get over your poor performance or embarrassing moment. This begs the question.. if not thinking about it doesn't lead to your desired result, what can you do instead that'll help you overcome your mistake?

There are many possible solutions out there, but one stands out above all others....and it's called the *Mindfulness* approach. You might have heard of the term Mindfulness at some point in your early career or possibly even on Television, as professional athletes are slowly realizing its potential. Phil Jackson (NBA coach winner of 11 championships with the Chicago Bulls and Los Angeles Lakers) is a popular figure who used mindfulness techniques with his players during practices, hence the nickname "Zen Master." Entire books and numerous articles have been written about mindfulness and several studies have been conducted showing its positive effects which are being recognized by sports organizations all around the world. To get to the point however...Mindfulness is simply a word to describe a state of mind where you allow yourself to experience any and all thoughts you have and simply choose to view them in a non-judgmental manner. You're able to accept that thoughts are neither good or bad, but simply a natural process of human life. Mindfulness allows you to experience the moment in its entirety, and allows you to accept whatever has happened. Specifically in terms of basketball, you need to understand that there will be ups and downs and no player is an exception to this no matter how good they might be. Mistakes are going to happen and in no way should you allow them to haunt you as you try and move forward with your career. So in the event that you find yourself engaging in Thought Suppression, quickly become aware and implement more of a Mindfulness perspective into your thought process. Your experience as a basketball athlete will undoubtedly become much more enjoyable and much more successful.

ental Workout

1. Next time you play in a game, try to keep track of the thoughts that impact your performance negatively. Write some of these thoughts down below.

2. Look at your list above. Are these thoughts a result of a negative experiences you've had in the past? Explain.

3. **How will you use the Mindfulness approach immediately to keep you from suppressing your thoughts?**

Competitive Anxiety

> *"YOU NEVER REACH YOUR FULL POTENTIAL BECAUSE YOU LET FEAR CONTROL YOUR THOUGHTS, AND THOSE FEARFUL THOUGHTS CREATE FEARFUL EMOTIONS, AND THOSE FEARFUL EMOTIONS LEAD TO FEARFUL ACTIONS."*

Mental Meltdown

The moment you've been waiting for is just moments away. Everything you have worked for this entire season is on the line. All those countless hours of practice, all those early morning workouts and late night film sessions, the blood, the sweat, the tears, all the pain, agony, and defeat...all leading up to this moment. The league championship game.

How are you feeling? Sweaty palms? Butterflies or knots in your stomach? Are you finding it difficult to stretch and get loose? Looking up into the stands realizing how many people are there to watch you play? Feeling the pressure of the moment?

Whether you're in a youth league or in the pros... young or old...a rookie or a veteran...competitive anxiety is experienced by every and all athletes at some point in their careers. And although experiencing some pre-game nerves is actually very normal, there are times where athletes become so overwhelmed that the anxiety cripples their thought process which in turn leads to a severe under performance.

But what exactly is this thought process? Well for starters, crippling anxiety is often a byproduct of an internal fear. This fear grabs control of the athlete's thoughts, and those fearful thoughts of course create fearful emotions, and those fearful emotions lead to fearful actions. It's a cycle that's very hard to break out of. But with the right training and mental approach you can limit the likelihood of experiencing high levels of competitive anxiety in the moments that mean the most to you and your team.

Definition and Examples

Competitive Anxiety- the nervous feeling you get before a big game, during a critical point in the game, and sometimes even after a game. Competitive anxiety is often something in your mind that you are "expecting" to happen, and that specific something causes you to be feel extremely nervous.

Along with Competitive Anxiety come two common outcomes, Fear of Failure and Choking Under Pressure.

1. *Fear of Failure*- an immense fear of taking chances, a fear of making mistakes, a fear of stepping outside of your comfort zone, a fear of losing, a fear of being unsuccessful, and a fear of the consequences that may follow.

   Example

   a. Sometimes at the end of practice coaches will allow players to shoot a free-throw. If made, practice is over. But if missed, the entire team has to run and do conditioning drills. Are you the one that steps up to shoot, or do you fall back with no desire to take on the pressure? Are you afraid of the consequences that come along with you missing the free throw?

2. *Choking (Choking Under Pressure)*- not performing as well as you normally do. In basketball, choking during crunch time is often associated with missing a game winning shot, missing free throws in a close game, turning the ball over in the final seconds, and "shrinking" or shying away in the biggest moments of a game.

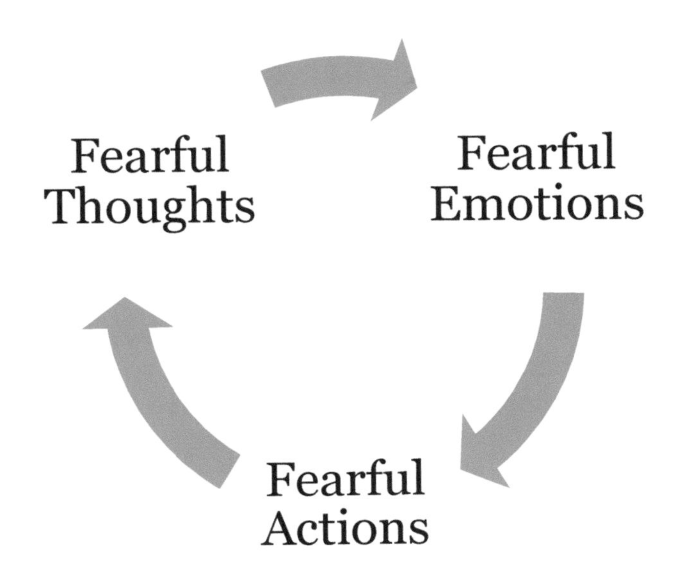

The Game Plan

So what can you do to stop competitive anxiety from ruining your basketball career? What can you do to no longer experience that fear of failure that's stopping you from reaching your potential? And how do you avoid choking in the moments where it matters most for you and your team?

The first thing you must do is identify what it is that makes you nervous, what it is that makes you scared, and what it is that makes you underperform. Some of the most common influences that lead to increased levels of competitive anxiety might come as a surprise to you: friends, family, and even coaches and teammates. How so? Many young athletes become completely fixated on what the opinion of others would be if they were to have a bad game. For example, what would your friends talk about at school the next day if you turned the ball over in the final minutes of a game? How disappointed would your family be if you choked at the free throw line and missed the opportunity to put your team ahead? How nervous would you be to go to practice the next day knowing that your coach and teammates are furious that you forgot the play during the final seconds of the fourth quarter? If these things have ran through your mind in the past, not to worry, you're not alone! What's important for you to realize is that none of these outcomes are actually real! That's right I'll say it again, they're NOT REAL. They are all just thoughts that come across your mind all stemming from...yup you guessed it... FEAR. If you stopped thinking about the consequences and only focused on the task at hand the emotional response in your body would completely change. This outlook would in turn lower the amount of anxiety you experience.

Now, in some cases, some players experience anxiety, fear of failure, and choke under pressure because they've had an unsuccessful experience in the past. And this is a little bit different because when a similar experience arises, those thoughts resurface bringing along with them all the negative emotions and feelings that previously crippled the athlete into underperforming. However, there's also a distinction that must be made here which will undoubtedly change the outcome for these athletes. And here it is...Instead of thinking of past failures as obstacles, as insurmountable mountains, as impossible challenges...athletes should instead think of those failures as opportunities to learn, as chances to correct a mistake, as a second wind to blow past the competition. In doing so it would again change their entire thought process which makes all the difference. It's all a matter of perspective. You've only lost if you allow yourself to lose. Every failure you experience is a challenge that you can learn from, and the ability to apply that lesson to your immediate future is crucial to reach the level of success you so badly desire.

Mental Workouts

1. List your 3 favorite NBA or WNBA players, go online and see what type of adversity and obstacles they have dealt with on the basketball court. How have they been criticized? What have they struggled with? How have they responded?

____

____

____

2. Now ask yourself the same questions above. How have you been criticized? What have you struggled with? How have you responded? And knowing what you know now, how would you respond differently?

Self- Talk

> *"SELF-TALK HAS BEEN SHOWN TO BE AN INCREDIBLY POWERFUL PSYCHOLOGICAL SKILL THAT IS USED BY SOME OF THE MOST SUCCESSFUL ATHLETES ON THE BASKETBALL COURT."*

ental Meltdown

"How could I be so stupid? Why did I not take that shot when I had the chance? Why do I continue to practice even though it seems like I'm not getting any better? Maybe I should just quit?"

The comments/questions above represent a point in time where an athlete hits a brick wall and begins to negatively evaluate himself/herself in a way that is completely unproductive. Whether it's after playing a bad game, making an in-game mistake, or committing an error during practice...athletes across all sports experience these moments as they are nearly unavoidable, but nonetheless difficult to get through. And overall very little is done by coaches and trainers to correct these negative self-evaluations, which of course makes it extremely difficult for the athlete to ever realize it's a huge problem and a horrible habit that works against their favor. This unwanted problem and habit in turn has a direct negative impact on the athlete's athletic performance.

This issue can be easily addressed by learning the mental skill (yes it is a skill), Self-Talk. And contrary to what you may believe...Self-Talk has been shown to be an incredibly powerful psychological skill that is used by some of the most successful athletes on the planet. There are some key distinctions however, so let's start by defining specifically what Self-Talk is and break it down into two different categories.

Definition & Examples

Self-Talk: speaking or talking to yourself out loud or in your thoughts.

Very straightforward. However, to ensure that athlete's aren't negatively evaluating themselves and their performance, these two types of Self-Talk have become prominent.

Positive Self-Talk: telling yourself words, phrases, and affirmations to motivate you and keep you focused on your target.

Example

1. When I get the ball on a 1 on 1 fastbreak, I tell myself, "You can't guard me." "I'm too fast." "I can easily score."
2. "Hard Work Beats Talent When Talent Doesn't Work Hard"- commonly used quote.

Instructional Self-Talk: telling yourself instructions to make sure you're accomplishing your desired expectation.

Example

1. When a shot goes up you can recite to yourself "turn and box out, stay low, and grab the rebound with both hands. Outlet the ball to a guard and sprint down court to get an easy bucket." Exactly how your coach instructs you to do it during practice.

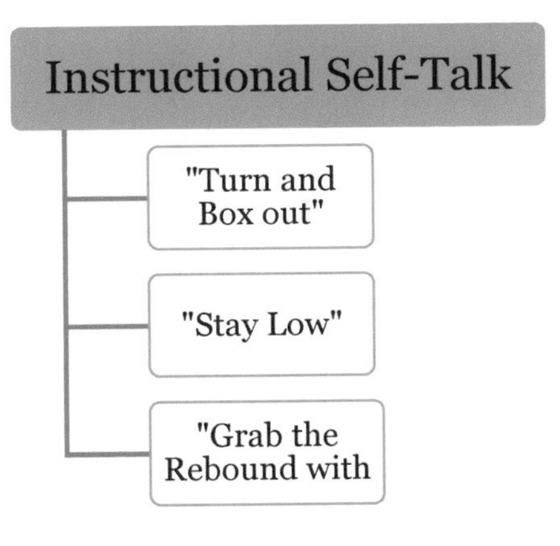

The Game Plan

It may seem strange to you that such a subtle change in the way you interpret and respond to your own behaviors and outcomes can make much of an impact on your athletic performance. But in reality, words are very powerful and really have a major influence in the way you view the world. Especially when we start considering how to deal with adversity, how to break through critical moments in your career, and how to continue to push when your gas tank is running on fumes...self-talk really becomes invaluable. A great example is non-other than Shaun Livingston of the Golden State Warriors. If you're not familiar with his story, during his early years with the Los Angeles Clippers Shaun suffered a freak injury on what seemed to be a routine basketball play. He tore 3 out of 4 ligaments in his knee, and his knee cap was completely dislocated...doctors even considered amputating his leg due to the severe damage he had suffered. It was gruesome. And as you can imagine, it was a very long road to recovery that really tested him both physically and psychologically.

And as you can guess...one of the key mental skills he relied on to help him in his rehab process was self-talk! If you get a chance to look up his story please do so it's truly very inspiring. He's documented saying that in certain moments he would tell himself "things could be worse"..."Ok, I'm making progress"..."I will play again." And slowly his thought process took a turn for the better... he went from believing he suffered a career ending injury to believing he had the ability to return to play in the NBA. Now in days, not only is he playing in the NBA but he's nearly an un-guardable force due to his size and athleticism and was a key component to the Warriors winning the NBA championship in the 2014-2015 season.

Lastly, whether you like the idea of using positive or instructional self-talk, my advice would be to use both, not one over the other. By using and developing both of these types of mental skills you certainly give yourself a huge edge over your opponents. It will allow you to prime your ability to stay focused which is really a lost art in todays' athletic world. In addition, it's highly recommended you start developing a "script." A script that you can use whenever you feel you need an extra boost in confidence or an extra push to get you over whatever hump you may be currently experiencing. Your script can come from anywhere, you can come up with it yourself or you can literally google "Motivational Quotes" and you'll find tons of short phrases that are designed to keep you focused and motivated. One thing is certain, you're going to be faced with great challenges throughout your career as a basketball player, no doubt about it. So it's best that when those challenges do arise and come your way you are ready to face them with the tools that'll give you the ability to overcome and conquer.

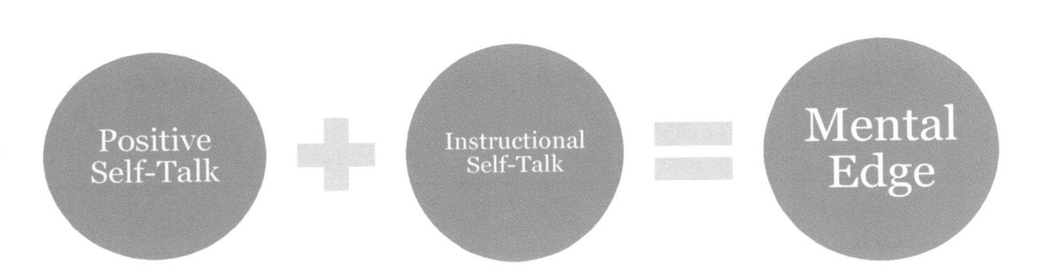

Mental Workout

1. Take some time and write down 10 words, phrases, and affirmations that get you focused. You can use anything that you've seen in a movie, read in a magazine, heard in a story, it can be something a friend has told you, advice from a teacher, whatever you'd like. Mix it up.

____

____

____

____

____

____

____

2. **Put yourself in a game situation and think about where you can use self-instruction. Write down examples of what you would say to yourself. Write down as many examples as you can.**

Zones of Optimal Performance

"REACHING A MENTAL ZONE IS DIFFICULT, BUT WHEN ACCOMPLISHED MANY BALLERS DESCRIBE THE EASE OF THE GAME, SHOOTING THE BALL FEELS LIKE THROWING A ROCK INTO THE OCEAN, AND EVERY MOVE BECOMES BUTTERY SMOOTH."

Mental Meltdown

Take a moment and think back to a time where you witnessed your favorite player perform at an all-time high level. From Steph Curry breaking the single game 3-point record, to Klay Thompson's 37 point quarter, to Kobe Bryant's 81 point game eruption, (just to mention a few) there's been countless performances where athletes just leave fans in sheer awe and amazement. Seemingly every shot they take seems to find the bottom of the net, every move they make seems to create the necessary space and separation for them to attack the basket, and everything just looks like they're ten steps ahead of everyone else. And what do all these feats have in common regardless of the athlete who is performing them? At any of the post-game interviews you will undoubtedly hear them say...

"I was in a ZONE."

Reaching this "Zone" is one of the most prized objectives to all athletes regardless of the sport that is being played. It's a state of mind where everything just starts to flow in their favor and things seem to come easy and natural. In basketball, many athletes describe the ease of the game, shooting the ball feels like throwing a rock into the ocean, and every move becomes buttery smooth. It's a beautiful thing to watch...and wouldn't it be more exciting if you as an athlete learned how you can reach this mental zone? Wouldn't it be great if you had the ability to replicate this phenomenon time and time again? Certainly your on court performances would sky rocket! So our goal here is for you to take away some tips that'll help you understand where your personal zone of optimal performance lies in order for you to have the ability to implement the necessary skills required to reach this mental state.

Definition & Example

Zone of Optimal Performance- the level of anxiety that you play best at, being able to reach a "mental zone", reaching a flow state, where everything just seems to come easy and you perform at your highest possible level athletically.

Example

1. During Kobe's 81-point performance against the Toronto Raptors it was evident from the start that he was in his own world. Every shot he took swished through the bottom of the net no matter how difficult the angle, and there was absolutely nothing the defense could do to stop him. During post-game interviews, Kobe shed some light as to what he felt like during his legendary performance... making comments such as "It's tough to explain"... "To sit here and say I grasp what has happened, that would be lying." It's almost as if he had an out of body experience as he was so locked in to doing whatever it took to win the game. Not even realizing that he was having one of the most remarkable nights in sports history.

The Game Plan

The possibilities of why Kobe Bryant was able to record one of the greatest scoring performances of all time are really endless (since he's one of those players that are not from planet earth). However, from a sports psychology perspective there are a lot of factors we can break down that can tell us how and why some players can reach a mental zone and a flow state that allow them to perform at an abnormally high level. Some of these factors include being able to play under pressure, being able to feel comfortable and relaxed, and getting over the fears of making mistakes during the course of a game.

At the end of the day, many of the different factors all lead to one road...Learning to cope with Anxiety. Take a look at the Chart that follows.

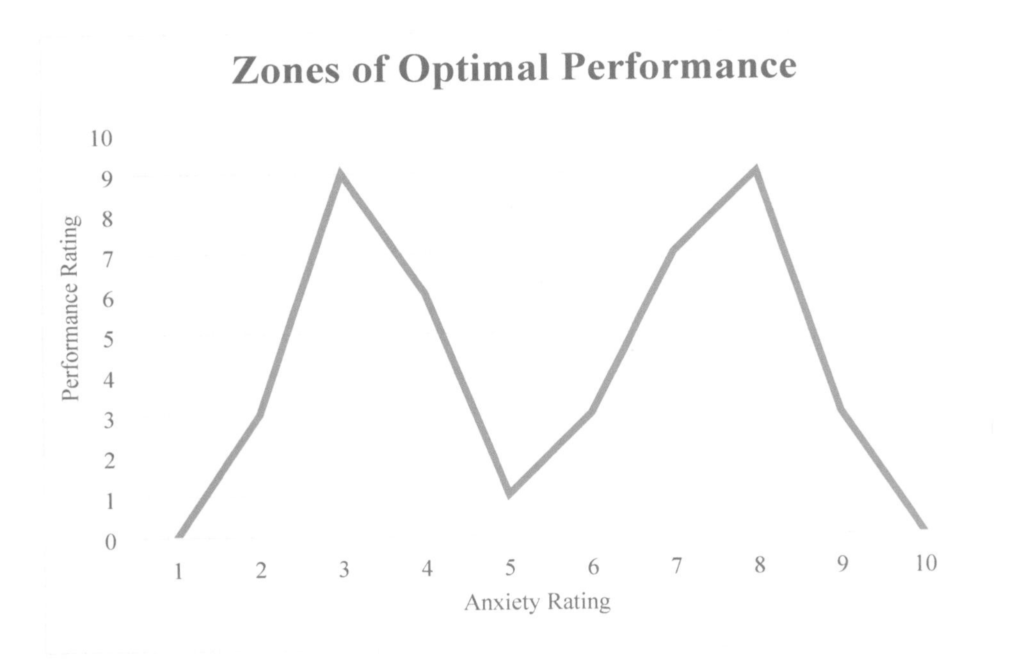

The chart above shows a rough average of where athletes feel they perform best at in terms of level of anxiety (nerves). As you can see (the two highest points), most players play at a high level when they are at an anxiety self-rating score of around 3 or a self-rating score of around 8. Scores near level 3 can best be described as moderately "low" anxiety while scores near level 8 can best be labeled as moderately "high" anxiety. And it all comes down to individual differences (personality, attitude, temperament, etc.). What does that mean? It means that some players simply prefer to play under moderately low levels of anxiety because that's where they can perform best at. It's a level where they feel comfortable, it's a level where they feel dominant, and it's a level where they feel in control. And the same reasons go for the other athletes who prefer to play under moderately high levels of anxiety. It's simply a matter of perspective and a matter of personal preference.

But let's consider the rest of the spectrum. Why don't players perform well at low anxiety self-ratings of 1 or high anxiety self-ratings of 10? Here's the answer...when players aren't nervous at all (anxiety self-rating of 1) they don't play well because they're not excited, they're not motivated to perform, and they're not engaged in the activity they are doing. They simply start to go through the motions. Can you imagine playing against a team of 2-year old's? Sure you would be the best player on the court, but it would be absolutely boring because it would be no contest! We all need to experience some level of nervousness to energize us and keep us focused. On the other hand, when players are really nervous (anxiety self-rating of 10) players panic, they psyche themselves out, and they start to freeze in the moment. Experiencing an enormous amount of anxiety all at once almost always leads to under-performing athletically. Not only that, but too much anxiety is also bad for your overall health, and can lead to a variety of different illnesses and mental health problems.

Now, after studying and learning the graph it's crucial for you to realize where you are along the spectrum. You have to know where you are in order to know how to progress and develop a "feel" for where your zone is. Are you a better performer under low levels of pressure and anxiety? Or do you prefer to feel higher levels of adrenaline when you play? Only you can answer that. Once you figure that out, it's important for you to try and control (harness) this feeling so you can mimic (copy) the feeling every time you play. For example, if you play at your best when you have moderately low anxiety, then do everything you can mentally and physically to get into that same mental state. Establishing a routine works great for this! Eating your favorite comfort food before a game...listening to your 10 favorite songs before a game...doing your favorite shooting drills before a game...there are many options. Finding what works for you will take some time and experimentation but will pay off greatly in the long run.

Mental Workout

1. I want you to think back to a time when you played at your absolute best. What did it feel like? Did you reach a mental "zone"? Was there a lot of pressure on you? How anxious or nervous were you before, during, and after the game?

2. Think back to a time when you played at your absolute worst. What did you feel? Was there a lot of pressure on you? How anxious or nervous were you before, during, and after the game?

3. Look back to your answers for questions 1 and 2. Do you notice any similarities between them? Do you notice any differences? What does this tell you about yourself?

4. What are some things you can do before your next game or before your next practice that will help put you in your zone of optimal performance? Also, go online and research the routines of your favorite basketball players. Are there some things that they do that you can use?

Attention

"WITH SO MANY FACTORS FIGHTING FOR YOUR ATTENTION YOU BECOME LIKE A SNIPER IN THE MIDDLE OF A WARZONE, YOU NEED TO BE ABLE TO FOCUS ALL OF YOUR ATTENTIVE ENERGY ON THE THINGS THAT MATTER MOST AT THAT VERY MOMENT."

Mental Meltdown

Tip off time! The ball goes up and your opponent gets the first possession. In the blink of an eye they get off to a fast start! A quick back door screen leads to an easy lay-up, and immediately upon scoring they jump into a full court press. One pass to you, you dribble toward the right side of the court, and as soon as you look up you're trapped. You try to make a pass to your teammate but the ball gets intercepted, and just like that another easy lay-up for the opposing team.

During the course of a basketball game there's an enormously large series of events going on all around you at the same time. You can practice as much as you possibly can, but there's simply nothing like playing in a real live game. You need to remember all the plays your coach taught you during practice, you need to stop the ball during defensive breakdowns, you need to react if someone drives down the lane and close out on the shooters when the ball is kicked out to the perimeter, you need to know what defense you're in, you need to know when a shot goes up so you can box out, and so on and so forth. It's very hard to keep up with it all. And not to mention that all this action is happening while your coach is yelling at you from the sidelines, your family and friends are screaming at you from the stands, and your teammates are all trying to get your attention whether they're on the court with you or on the bench. With so many factors fighting for your attention you become like a sniper in the middle of a warzone, you need to be able to focus all of your attentive energy on the things that matter most at that very moment.

Definition and Examples

Divided Attention- trying to pay equal attention to many things at the same time (multitasking). Because your attention is divided, you don't perform as well as you would if you gave your full attention to one thing at a time.

Example

1. Defending on ball screens is one of the biggest challenges of any player and team. It's difficult because decisions need to be made in a split second, communication needs to be on point, and the game plan needs to be very well understood as the way you defend one player may be different than the way you defend another player (shooter vs penetrator). Your attention must be laser like, as one small mistake can lead to a complete lapse of the defense which of course leads to an easy bucket.

a. *Inattentional Blindness*- this term explains the phenomenon of you not being able to see something that is very easily visible (obvious). You're unable to see it because of your lack of attention.

Example

1. When your coach instructs you stick to the player you're guarding like white on rice, and you become fixated on doing exactly that. The next play down, your teammate falls and the opposing player he's guarding cuts to the front of the rim. In plain view everyone can see that the opposing player is Wide Open, but you're so fixated on sticking to your assignment that you don't see anything else going on around you.

Selective Attention- being able to filter out information that isn't important, and focusing on the information that is important.

Example

1. While shooting a free throw, being able to zone out all of the distractions and focusing on putting the ball in the basket.

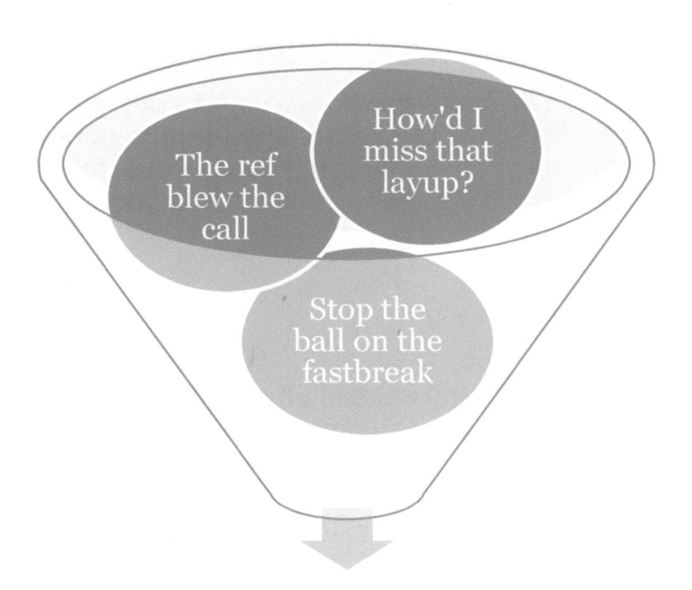

STOP THE BALL!!!

The Game Plan

The diagram above is a perfect depiction of how your mind can act like a filter or funnel during a game. Picture this: you drive hard to the basket, get contact from the defender, think the ref is going to call a foul, but there's no whistle at the end of the play and you blow the layup. Worse, now the other team is on a fast break looking for an easy basket. In this situation it's easy to get distracted and divide your attention on how you should've got the call on the previous play or how you should've made the layup. But what you should really be focusing your attention on is getting back on defense and stopping the ball to slow down the fast break opportunity! It's just that simple. Yet so many times players get caught up into thinking how bad the refs are, or how much trash the other team is talking, or how the fans are being disrespectful. And when players get caught up with all the non-sense and different scenarios instead of being in the moment, that's when they end up under performing and getting benched. Don't let this be you.

Instead, utilize Selective Attention to zone in on the things that are most important in that moment, whether it's practice or a game. Don't become a victim of divided attention and waste your attentive energy on multiple things that won't even help you perform at a higher level. And this doesn't only apply to basketball, think back to when you took your last algebra test, or your last biology exam... How many times did you catch yourself being distracted by something else that was completely unrelated to what you were doing.. like what you should eat for lunch, or what you're going to wear to the party, or how much clothes you should pack for your upcoming vacation? It happens to the best of us, and it's extremely unproductive. So understand that being able to focus on one thing at a time will enable you to give 100% effort on that one task, which will allow you to do it much more effectively and much more efficiently, leading to a much improved overall athletic performance.

Mental Workouts

1. Can you think of a game situation that you've encountered where you were asked to divide your attention on several different tasks? How did you feel? How did you perform?

____

____

____

____

____

____

____

____

____

2. Knowing what you know now, how can you use your attention more effectively?

Self-Confidence

"YOU ARE THE ARCHITECT, YOU CAN BUILD YOURSELF UP HIGH LIKE A SKYSCRAPER OR YOU CAN SET A FLIMSY FOUNDATION THAT CAN COLLAPSE AT ANY MOMENT."

ental Meltdown

It's the 4th quarter, no time left on the clock, your team is down by one point...and guess who's on the free throw line??? That's right. YOU.

It's the most critical point in the game, a moment where you have the chance and power to dictate how the game ends. You can make two free throws and win the game, you can make one free throw to tie the game and send it into overtime, or you can miss both and lose. What is the one thing every basketball athlete wished they had in this situation? SUPREME SELF-CONFIDENCE!

And yes...Confidence (or self-confidence) is one of the most important factors linked to the amount of success an athlete experiences throughout the course of their career. Why? The psychological and physical relationship is simple, the more confident you are mentally as a basketball player, the more likely you are to physically succeed and play well. No matter how short you are, no matter how slow you are, no matter how untalented people say you are, if you're confident in your abilities you have a great chance of keeping up and playing with the best of them.

At the end of the day you are the architect, you can build your confidence up high like a skyscraper or you can set forth a flimsy foundation that can collapse at any moment. In other words, you are in charge of the level of self-confidence you hold within you...it really is all in your head! But if you lack the ability to build your confidence up, what happens is that as soon as you encounter a challenge or any type of adversity you will surely be unprepared and unequipped to deal with the added pressures that come along. So let's get a deeper understanding of what self-confidence really is and consider all the different factors that can influence the level of confidence you play with.

efinition & Example

Confidence- having a strong belief in yourself and in your abilities.

Example

1. I'm confident that I'm the best player in the league this season.

A statement that is very easily said, but that can be very difficult to prove. Especially as we consider the following confidence pitfalls:

If you are extremely quick but suffer a slightly sprained ankle, would you still have confidence in your speed? If you miss 10 three pointers in a row during a game, would you still have confidence in your shooting ability at the end of the game? If your coach tells you you're not good enough to make the starting line-up, how confident would you be about your talents and abilities moving forward? There's too many confidence killing scenarios to name them all...what's important is to learn how to build and sustain high levels of confidence so that when your moment comes you are ready to perform at a high level.

The Game Plan

Here's lesson number one... there is a direct relationship between the amount of time you practice and the amount of confidence that you play with. In other words, the more you practice the more confidence you will ultimately have. But pay close attention, when you're practicing and working on your skills you must ALWAYS start at the most BASIC LEVEL. Why? Because it's important to build a solid foundation before attempting to blossom your game to levels that you're unprepared for. For example, you might be guilty (as so many players are) of running onto the court during warm ups only to head straight to the three-point line and start shooting up bricks at the rim. Bad idea!

Instead, what you should do is start by shooting from 2ft away, and then 4ft away, and then 10ft away, and then 15ft away, and then finally three-pointers. It should be more of a steady progression further and further out into the perimeter as you continue to get a feel for your jump shot and see the ball go through the net. Running straight to the three-point line and seeing yourself miss jumper after jumper will only result in you feeling tentative and thinking "Damn I'm Off Today."

And it's not just jump shots. Ball handling, passing, defense, and any skill building activity for that matter should begin with the most simple and basic drills. A good example of this is Steph Curry's pre-game shooting and ball handling routines. As you've probably observed, even though he's one of the best ball handlers and shooters in the world, he doesn't deviate away from doing his basic dribbling and shooting workouts before each and every game.

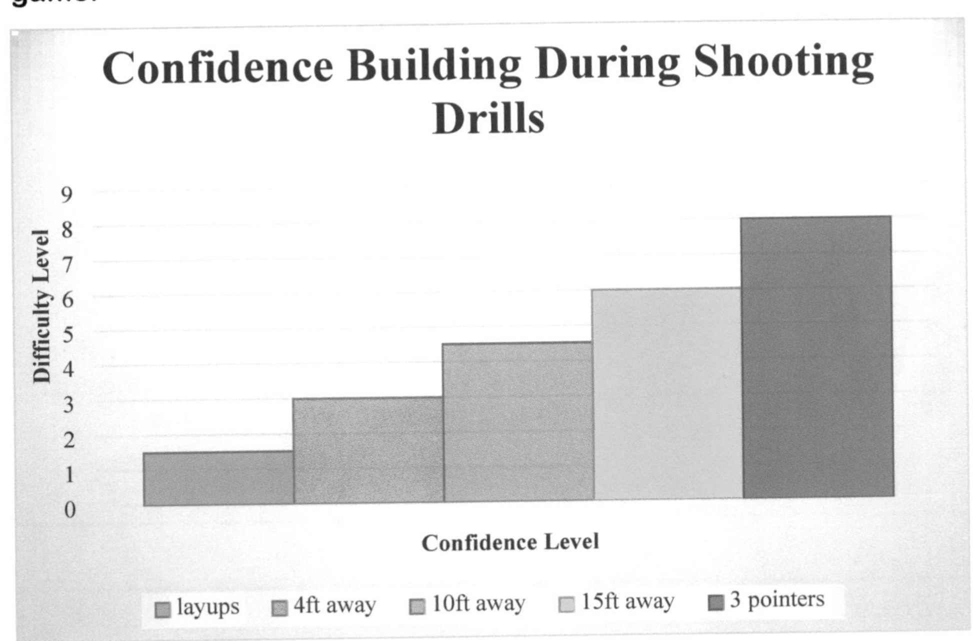

This leads us directly into lesson number two, Be a Student of the Game. Study the skills and movements of college and professional basketball players, or any player that is better than you for that matter. Watching someone who's better than you and being able to break down what they do in order to implement facets of their game into yours can be a huge confidence booster because you already know that what they're doing works. After all, they're better than you for a reason right? Mimicking these players is almost (and yes I said Almost) like having a short cut to success. They've put in years and years of hard work to develop and hone in on their skills and moves, and all you have to do is learn how to execute those moves yourself. Pro ballers do this all the time, just look at how Kobe Bryant patterned his game after Michael Jordan as a young player. If you were to play highlights of both players side by side simultaneously, it would be like watching the same player but in different bodies and jerseys. Great players constantly learn from other great players and simply follow the same path to success.

And finally lesson number three, and I can't stress it enough, is stay mentally resilient. As a basketball player, you are bound to be faced with adversity, you're bound to be faced with difficulties, and you are bound to make mistakes. That's just the nature of basketball. What makes the difference and what you need to concentrate on is how you react, how you bounce back, and how you are going to be better after the fact. As we've made this point before, no one has control over your thoughts and perception but YOURSELF. So keep grinding and don't let any outside noise interfere with your laser focus toward accomplishing your goals and aspirations.

ental Workouts

1. Think of a time when you played with supreme confidence. Why did you play so confident? What were you thinking about? What was the outcome?

____

____

____

2. Now do the opposite. Think of a time when you played with absolutely no confidence. Why didn't you have confidence? What was going through your mind? What was the outcome?

3. **Analyze what you wrote for the two questions above. What can you do to play with confidence all the time? On the other hand, what can you do to avoid losing your confidence during a game?**

Coming Back from Injury

> *"WHAT MOST ATHLETES FAIL TO REALIZE IS THAT THE PHYSICAL PAIN IS INTENSE, BUT TOLERABLE, IT'S THE PSYCHOLOGICAL PAIN THAT BECOMES ALMOST UNBEARABLE TO DEAL WITH."*

Mental Meltdown

It's Saturday morning and your coach sends a text to the entire team...he's decided to have an early shoot around in order to prepare for the upcoming tournament the next day. Nothing intense, just an opportunity for everyone to get some shots up and go over the game plan. A really light practice (and a dream come true)! Everything runs smoothly, and since there's nothing else to do once practice is over, you and a couple of your teammates decide to head over to the park to play some pick-up games (despite your coach's advisement against it).

So you go to the park with your teammates and immediately you're able to get a game going. Should be an easy win right? Slowly but surely, the game begins to get intense and everyone starts to play harder and harder. Next thing you know on a routine basketball play you go up for a rebound, and on your way down you land directly on an opponent's foot. Just like that...you suffer a severe left ankle sprain and are out indefinitely for at least the next two weeks. No tournament for you!

Whether you like it or not, injury is a natural part of basketball. The sport itself takes place on 94 feet of hardwood, solid concrete if you're outdoors, with 10 players all competing for possession of one single basketball. With intensity rising at every level and with every player trying their hardest to win, someone is bound to get hurt or injured at some point even though it's unintentional. There's just too many things going on at the same time and risky situations all around. It's rare that any serious basketball athlete in the world escapes the injury bug entirely. And although we hope and pray for every player to have a good healthy career throughout, it's best that everyone is prepared and becomes equipped with the mental skills that are necessary to deal with and cope with the psychological and physical symptoms of an injury. From minor sprains to severely torn ligaments and broken bones, it's tough recovering and coming back at full strength. What most athletes fail to realize is that the physical pain is intense, but tolerable, it's the psychological pain that becomes almost unbearable to deal with.

"MY BODY COULD STAND THE CRUTCHES BUT MY MIND COULDN'T STAND THE SIDELINE"

- **MICHAEL JORDAN**

efinition & Example

Injury- being harmed physically, emotionally, and or psychologically.

Example

1. Injuries come in all shapes and sizes. In basketball, some of the most common injuries include, sprained ankles, jammed fingers, torn ligaments in the knees, pulled hamstrings and calf muscles, and lower back pain (just to name a few).

Now, when most athletes suffer from an injury they tend to focus on the physical injury itself. There may be a lot of swelling, significant muscle tightness, and overall the body needs time and rest in order to be able to fully recover. But the biggest downfall about this is that by not paying attention to the psychological aspects that an injury brings along with it...many athletes return from a serious injury when they truly aren't fully prepared or ready, and their performance on the basketball court suffers greatly. When an athlete isn't psychologically ready to return from an injury their thoughts are completely occupied on all the things that can possibly go wrong. They become afraid of re injury while driving to the basket for a lay-up, they become tentative in the moves that they make while trying to break a full-court press, they begin to second guess themselves and their ability while taking a jump shot, and they become scared to make that quick cut to the basket while on a fast break opportunity.

Physical Recovery	Swelling Muscle Tightness Pain
Psychological Recovery	Frustration Decrease in Confidence Decrease in Motivation

The Game Plan

When it comes to injury, your primary concern should be of course PREVENTION. Wear protective gear like padding and ankle braces, and make sure to warm-up and stretch properly before any physical activity. This way, the chances of you suffering a serious or severe injury will be significantly reduced. Which of course will save you a ton of pain and frustration in the future.

However in the event that you do suffer an injury, how can you recover in the fastest time possible both physically and psychologically? Well in terms of psychological recovery, in most instances the number one thing you will need to change in order to recover is your perception (the way you think about it). Many of today's young athletes make the unconscious decision to view their injury as an unfixable problem, as a mountain high obstacle, and as the end of their season or career. This in large part is due to many of the critics out there who make these insane claims that when certain injuries take place the athletes who have suffered them will never return to their old selves. That somehow, because of these injuries it becomes "impossible" to ever return to full strength... and athletes that choose to believe and perceive their personal situations this way actually recover the slowest and have the most difficult and painful recovery processes. How so? Well as we've mentioned before thoughts have an immense and direct impact on the body and how it responds. With that being said, as you've probably already guessed by now is that athletes who make the decision to view their injury as a challenge to get better, as a learning opportunity, as a chance to become smarter and stronger than before, and as a way to silence their doubters and critics once and for all are the ones who actually recover more quickly, efficiently, and effectively. So first you must re-frame your thoughts!

Secondly and importantly, it's necessary to have social support. For some of us I know it's extremely difficult to admit we need help let alone ask for help. But in terms of injury recovery it's crucial to have people around you that can support you when times get hard and when you start to get down on yourself, because at the end of the day the road will be tough! And in certain cases it may even be beneficial for you to seek help and support from those who are not associated in any way with your basketball career, like coaches, trainers, or teammates. Why? Sometimes, but not always, people who are tied to your basketball career may unintentionally put your athletic interest and ability first instead of your health and wellness. Meaning that they push and encourage you to return to the court regardless if you feel you're ready and recovered or not. Especially in youth sports, we often hear negative comments like "just suck it up, just walk it off, it's not that bad stop being a sissy..?" This is horrible advice. Not only do comments like these negatively impact an athletes psyche but they also leave athletes vulnerable to re-injury if they attempt to return to play too soon.

Last but not least, a huge part of injury recovery must involve the mental skills you have learned in the previous exercises:

mental imagery, positive/instructional self-talk, and goal setting. This is a perfect time for you to tie it all together. Visualizing yourself getting stronger every day, one step closer to full recovery, and setting short term goals to make sure you're reaching your target. You already know the science behind it, so I'll let you be creative and come up with your own mental skills plan.

Mental Workouts

1. Think about a time when you've been injured. What was your initial reaction? How did your reaction change over time? What was your recovery process like?

____

____

____

____

____

____

____

____

____

____

____

____

____

____

2. **Knowing what you know now, what would you do differently? How do you think your recovery process would have been different?**

CPSIA information can be obtained
at www.ICGtesting.com
Printed in the USA
LVHW071612040122
707833LV00001B/9

* 9 7 8 1 5 4 2 7 6 4 2 7 8 *